CANADA

Maria Koran and
John Willis

EYEDISCOVER

Go to **www.eyediscover.com** and enter this book's unique code.

BOOK CODE

AVA23366

EYEDISCOVER brings you optic readalongs that support active learning.

Published by AV2
276 5th Avenue, Suite 704 #917
New York, NY 10001
Website: www.eyediscover.com

Library of Congress Control Number: 2021937093

ISBN 978-1-7911-4202-5 (hardcover)

Printed in Guangzhou, China
1 2 3 4 5 6 7 8 9 0 25 24 23 22 21

042021
102120

Project Coordinator: John Willis
Designer: Mandy Christiansen

The publisher acknowledges Getty Images and Shutterstock as the primary image suppliers for this title.

CANADA

In this book, you will learn about

- where it is
- who lives there
- what it is known for

and much more!

Canada is one of the largest countries on Earth. Only Russia has more land.

More than 38 million people live in Canada.

Canada has many cities. More people live in Toronto than in any other Canadian city.

Canada

Ottawa is the capital city of Canada. It is where the country's leader lives and works.

Yukon
Northwest Territories
Nunavut
British Columbia
Alberta
Saskatchewan
Manitoba
Ontario
Quebec
Newfoundland and Labrador
New Brunswick

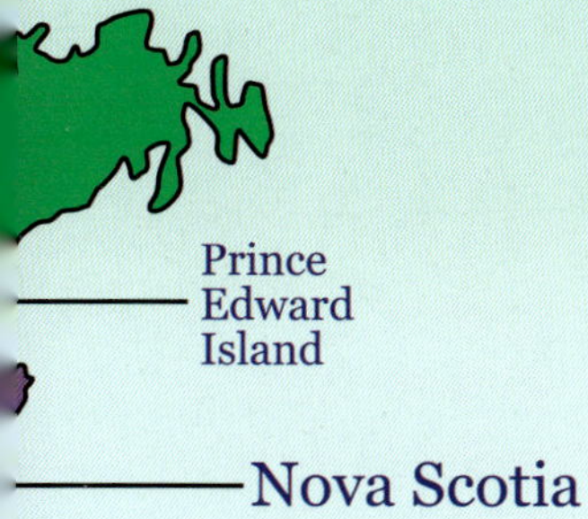

Canada has 10 provinces and 3 territories. Ontario is the province with the most people.

STOP
ARRÊT

Canada has two main languages. They are English and French.

There are many symbols of Canada. Canada's flag is red and white with a maple leaf in its center.

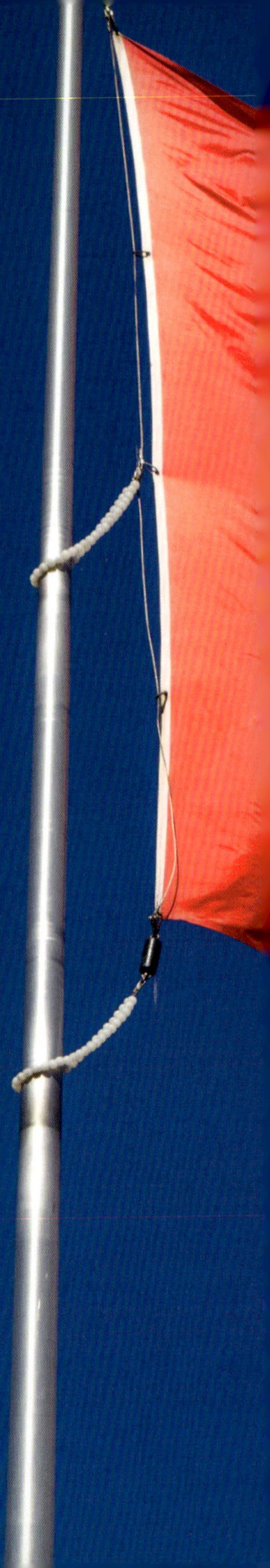

Another Canadian symbol is the beaver. It is the country's national animal.

Canada is known for its many lakes. There are more than 2 million lakes in the country.

CANADA BY THE NUMBERS

Great Bear Lake is the **LARGEST** lake found **entirely in Canada.** It is the **eighth-largest** lake on **Earth.**

Canada has **two national sports. HOCKEY** is the national **winter sport. LACROSSE** is the national **summer sport.**

The **Toronto** area has more than **6 MILLION** people.

Canada's **national flag** was introduced in **1965**.

A **beaver** can weigh more than **70 POUNDS** (32 kilograms).

Canada and the **United States** share the **LONGEST** **border** on **Earth** between two countries.

KEY WORDS

Research has shown that as much as 65 percent of all written material published in English is made up of 300 words. These 300 words cannot be taught using pictures or learned by sounding them out. They must be recognized by sight. This book contains 35 common sight words to help young readers improve their reading fluency and comprehension. This book also teaches young readers several important content words, such as proper nouns. These words are paired with pictures to aid in learning and improve understanding.

Page	Sight Words First Appearance
4	Earth, has, is, land, more, of, on, one, only, the
6	in, live, people, than
9	any, city, many, other
11	and, country, it, where, works
13	most, with
15	are, they, two
16	a, its, there, white
19	animal, another
20	for

Page	Content Words First Appearance
4	Canada, Russia
9	Toronto
11	capital city, leader, Ottawa
12	Alberta, British Columbia, Manitoba, New Brunswick, Newfoundland and Labrador, Northwest Territories, Nunavut, Ontario, Quebec, Saskatchewan, Yukon
13	Nova Scotia, Prince Edward Island, provinces, territories
15	English, French, languages
16	center, flag, maple leaf, symbols
19	beaver
20	lakes

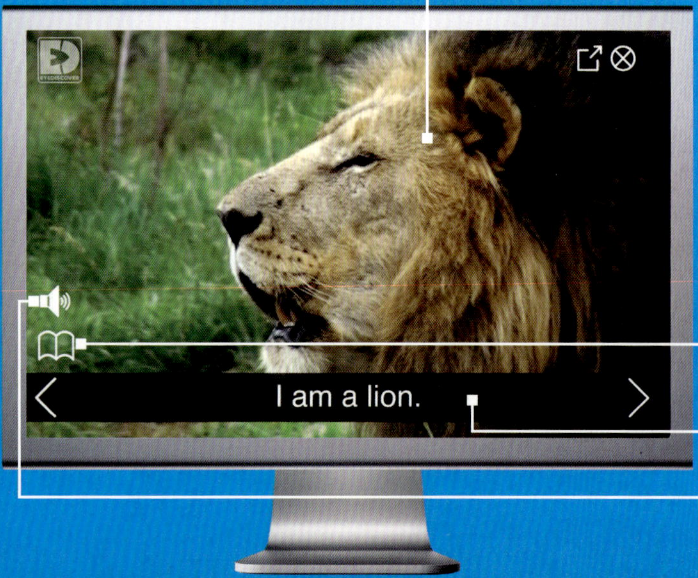

Watch
Video content brings each page to life.

Browse
Thumbnails make navigation simple.

Read
Follow along with text on the screen.

Listen
Hear each page read aloud.

EYEDISCOVER

Go to www.eyediscover.com and enter this book's unique code.

BOOK CODE

AVA23366